C000172681

DASH Diet

Cookbook

Discover the Power of Dash Diet with Delicious and Healthy Recipes

Jane Clark

© **Copyright 2021 by Jane Clark- All rights reserved.**

The following Book is reproduced below with the goal of providing information that is as accurate and reliable as possible. Regardless, purchasing this Book can be seen as consent to the fact that both the publisher and the author of this book are in no way experts on the topics discussed within and that any recommendations or suggestions that are made herein are for entertainment purposes only. Professionals should be consulted as needed prior to undertaking any of the action endorsed herein.

This declaration is deemed fair and valid by both the American Bar Association and the Committee of Publishers Association and is legally binding throughout the United States.

Furthermore, the transmission, duplication, or reproduction of any of the following work including specific information will be considered an illegal act irrespective of if it is done electronically or in print. This extends to creating a secondary or tertiary copy of the work or a recorded copy and is only allowed with the express written consent from the Publisher. All additional right reserved.

The information in the following pages is broadly considered a truthful and accurate account of facts and as such, any inattention, use, or misuse of the information in question by the reader will render any resulting actions solely under their purview. There are no scenarios in which the publisher or the original author of this work can be in any fashion deemed liable for any hardship or damages that may befall them after undertaking information described herein.

Additionally, the information in the following pages is intended only for informational purposes and should thus be thought of as universal. As befitting its nature, it is presented without assurance regarding its prolonged validity or interim quality. Trademarks that are mentioned are done without written consent and can in no way be considered an endorsement from the trademark holder.

Table of Contents

Introduction

I would like to thank you for getting this DASH Diet Cookbook.

The DASH Diet was created by a branch of the US Department of Health and Human Services. DASH stands for Dietary Approaches to Stop Hypertension.

The DASH diet is a diet that was developed to help reduce high blood pressure. It is for this reason that the foods that can be consumed in this diet are low in sodium.
The diet is clear and simple:
- Consume more fruits, vegetables and low-fat dairy products.
- Reduce foods with high levels of trans fat, saturated fat and cholesterol.
- Consume foods with whole grains, seafood, nuts and poultry.
- Limit salt, red meat, sweets, and sugary drinks.
The safe strategy of the DASH diet is to minimize blood pressure without medicines.

We have researched and collected the most amazing Dash diet recipes for you to try with the ingredients you're allowed to eat!

So, let's get this wonderful experience started! Have fun and enjoy the Dash lifestyle!

8

Chapter 1: Smoothies Recipes

1. Oat Cocoa Smoothie

Preparation time: 10 minutes

Cook time: 5 minutes

Total time: 15

Serving: 1

Ingredients:

- 1 tsp of vanilla extract

- Skim milk: 3/4 cup

- Half cup of plain low-fat yogurt

- Ground flaxseed: 1 tbsp.

- 1 small banana

- Unsweetened cocoa powder: 1 tsp

- Quick-cook oats: 1/4 cup

- Dash of ground cinnamon

Instructions:

- In a blender, add all ingredients

- Blend until smooth.

- Add more milk if required.

- Serve and enjoy.

Nutrition per serving: 350 calories| 19 g protein|5 g fat| 1 g saturated fat|60 g carbohydrates|7 g fiber| 6 mg cholesterol| 177 mg sodium

2. Tropical Green Breakfast Smoothies

Preparation time: 10 minutes

Cook time: 5 minutes

Total time: 15

Serving: 2

Ingredients:

- Chunks of 1 banana
- One cup of baby spinach
- 1/4 cup of plain Greek yogurt
- Pineapple chunks: 1 cup
- Pineapple juice or water: 1/4 cup
- 1/3 cup of oats
- Chunks: 1 big mango

Instructions:

- In a blender, add all ingredients.
- Blend until smooth.
- Add more milk if required.
- Serve

Nutrition Per Serving: 265 calories| protein 6 g |carbohydrates 32.3 g |fat 3.4 g| cholesterol 7.5 mg |sodium 21.4 mg

3. Green Apple Smoothie

Preparation time: 10 minutes

Cook time: 5 minutes

Total time:

Serving: 2

Ingredients:

- Apple cider: 1 cup

- One small banana

- Kale: 1–2 cups, stems removed

- Pinch of cinnamon

- Green apple cut into chunks: one cup

- Water or ice: 1 cup

Instructions:

- In a blender, add all ingredients

- Blend until smooth.

- Add more milk if required.

- Serve

Nutrition Per Serving: Calories 233|Total Fat 0.5g|Sodium 31.7mg|Total Carbohydrate 56.4g|Dietary Fiber 3.6g|sugars 30.8g| Protein 2g

Chapter 2: Breakfast Recipes

1. Fruit Pizza

Preparation time: 10 minutes

Cook time: 30 minutes

Total time: 40 minutes

Serving: 2

Ingredients:

- Blueberries: 2 tablespoons

- 1 whole-grain muffin

- Sliced strawberries: 2 tablespoons

- Chopped pineapple: 2 tablespoons

- Cream cheese, fat-free: 2 tablespoons

Instructions:

- Half the English muffin and toast to your liking.

- Add cream cheese on each half.

- Top with fruits as you like on top of cream cheese.

- Serve right away.

Nutrition per serving: 77 calories|0.4 g carbohydrate |0 g saturated fat| 0 mg cholesterol| 6 g fat |54 mg sodium| 7g sugars|9 g protein|

2. Tofu Scramble

Preparation time: 10 minutes

Cook time: 30 minutes

Total time: 40 minutes

Serving: 2

Ingredients:

- 2 cups of kale roughly chopped
- One cup of extra-firm tofu
- half red pepper, cut into slices
- Olive oil: 1-2 Tbsp.
- 1/4 onion, cut into slices

Sauce:

- Half tsp of ground cumin
- 1/8 tsp of sea salt
- 1/4 tsp of chili powder
- Water
- Half tsp of garlic powder

Instructions:

- Dry the tofu, wrap in a clean towel, and place a heavy skillet on top for at least 15 minutes.

- In the meantime, add dry spices in a bowl and mix with water to make a sauce. Set it aside.

- Sauté onion, red pepper in olive oil for five minutes. Add a pinch of salt and pepper.

- Add kale and steam for two minutes.

- Crumble tofu in small pieces.

- Add tofu on one side of the vegetable pan. Cook for two minutes, then add the sauce. Mix everything.

- Serve hot.

Nutrition per serving: Calories 212|Carbohydrates: 7.1 g| Protein: 16.4 g| Fat: 15.1 g| Saturated Fat: 2.4 g| Polyunsaturated Fat: 4.8 g| Monounsaturated Fat: 7 g| Cholesterol: 0 mg| Sodium: 600 mg| Potassium: 376 mg| Fiber: 2.1 g| Sugar: 3.3 g

3. Mushroom Spinach Omelette Recipe

Preparation time: 10 minutes

Cook time: 10 minutes

Total time: 20 minutes

Serving: 4

Ingredients:

- 5 mushrooms, cut into slices
- Olive oil: 1 tablespoon
- Sliced onion: 1/4 cup
- 2 tbsp. Of goat cheese
- One egg + 2 egg whites
- Fresh spinach: 1 and a half cups

Instructions:

- Sauté onion in olive oil for 2-3 minutes, until translucent
- Add mushroom slices to the pan, cook for 4 to 5 minutes, until slightly browned.
- Add spinach, cook until wilted add pepper and salt. Set it aside.
- In a greased skillet, cook the whisked eggs until slightly set.
- Add mushroom mix to eggs and top with goat cheese.

- Fold the other half over the mushroom mix.
- Cook for 30 seconds.
- Garnish with green onions

Nutrition per serving: Serving Size: 1 omelette: Calories: 412|Sugar: 8 g| Sodium: 332 mg| Fat: 29 g| Carbohydrates: 18 g| Fiber: 4 g| Protein: 25 g| Cholesterol: 199 mg|

4. Eggs & Tomato Breakfast Melts

Preparation time: 10 minutes

Cook time: 10 minutes

Total time: 20 minutes

Serving: 4

Ingredients:

- Olive oil: 1 teaspoon

- Two English muffins, whole-grain, cut in half

- 8 whisked egg whites

- 4 scallions, finely sliced

- Salt, a pinch

- Half cup of Swiss cheese, shredded, reduced-fat

- Black pepper, to taste

- Half cup of cherry tomatoes, quartered

Instructions:

- Toast the muffins halves as you like.

- Sauté 3 scallions for 2-3 minutes. Add salt, egg whites, pepper and cook.

- Add this egg mix to the toasted muffin, add cheese, tomato slices, and scallions.

- Let the cheese melt in the broiler for one minute.

- Serve hot.

Nutrition per serving: Calories 301|Sugar: 8 g| Sodium: 123 mg| Fat: 9 g| Carbohydrates: 11.1 g| Protein: 12.2 g| Cholesterol: 4 mg|

5. Crunchy Avocado Toast

Preparation time: 10 minutes

Cook time: 10 minutes

Total time: 20 minutes

Serving: 1

Ingredients:

- Red pepper flakes
- Brown rice cakes: 2, unsalted
- Half small avocado, mashed
- One Small tomato, cut into slices

Instructions:

- Spread the mashed avocado over rice cakes.
- Add tomato slices, and top with a pinch of salt and pepper flakes.

Nutrition per serving: Calories 201|Sugar: 8 g| Sodium: 121 mg| Fat: 9 g| Carbohydrates: 11.0 g| Protein: 12.2 g| Cholesterol: 4 mg|

Chapter 3: Poultry & Meat Recipes

1. Chicken with Celery Root Puree

Preparation time: 10 minutes

Cook time: 45 minutes

Total time: 55 minutes

Serving: 4

Ingredients:

- Apple juice: 2/3 cup, unsweetened
- 4 skinless, boneless chicken breasts cut into halves
- Half teaspoon of freshly ground black pepper
- Canola oil: 3 teaspoons divided
- 2 cloves of minced garlic
- 1/4 teaspoon of sea salt
- One celery root, peeled: 3 cups chopped
- Butternut squash: 2 cups peeled, chopped
- One small diced onion

Instructions:

- Season the chicken breast with salt and pepper.

- In a pan, add tsp. of oil and brown the chicken breast on each side; on medium flame, turn off the heat and set it aside.

- In the same skillet, add the rest of the oil, sauté onion, celery root, squash, cook until squash becomes tender crispy. Add garlic, cook for one minute.

- Add chicken back to the skillet, add unsweetened apple juice, let it boil, turn heat low and cover it, let it simmer for 12 to 15 minutes until an inserted thermometer reads 165.

- Take chicken out and keep in a warm oven. Cook the vegetables and puree in a food processor. Heat it well in the same pan.

- Serve with chicken.

Nutrition per serving: one half of chicken breast + 2/3 cup of vegetable puree: calories 328|94mg cholesterol| 8g fat |348mg sodium| 28g carbohydrate | 37g protein |10g sugars| 1g saturated fat| 5g fiber

2. Beef & Black Bean Spaghetti Squash

Preparation time: 10 minutes

Cook time: 30 minutes

Total time: 40 minutes

Serving: 4

Ingredients:

- One spaghetti squash, medium-sized
- Half cup of diced red onion
- Yellow mustard: 2 tablespoons
- Plain Greek yogurt: 1/4 cup
- One can of (15 ounces) black beans, no-salt-added, drained and rinsed
- 3/4 pounds of lean ground beef
- Chopped fresh kale: 2 cups
- Any hot sauce: 2 to 3 teaspoons
- 4 cloves of minced garlic

Instructions:

- Trim the squash, and cut in half, takeout the middle part. Add cut squash to pressure cooker with one cup of water. Lock the lid and cook on high for seven minutes. The other way is to microwave for 15-20 minutes.

- In a pan, sauté onion, beef over medium flame, until meat is browned, for 4 to 6 minutes. Drain it, then add garlic, hot sauce cooks for one more minute. Add in the kale and black beans, cook for 2 to 3 minutes.

- With a fork, shred the spaghetti squash. Mix with meat.

- Serve with plain Greek yogurt.

Nutrition per serving: 1-half cups: calories 401|314mg sodium| 12g fat |4g saturated fat|2g sugars| 57mg cholesterol| 13g fiber| 26g protein|51g carbohydrate|

3. Pork & Orzo

Preparation time: 10 minutes

Cook time: 30 minutes

Total time: 40 minutes

Serving: 6

Ingredients:

- 12 cups of water
- 1 and a half pounds of pork tenderloin
- One fresh package of (6 ounces) baby spinach
- Extra virgin olive oil: 2 tablespoons
- Grape tomatoes: 1 cup, cut into halves

- Roughly ground pepper: 1 teaspoon

- 1 and 1/4 cups of orzo pasta, uncooked

- Salt: 1/4 teaspoon

- Feta cheese, crumbled: 3/4 cup

Instructions:

- Add pepper to pork, cut into one-inch cubes. In a pan, add olive oil, pork and cook for 8 to 10 minutes, until it is no longer pink.

- In a Dutch oven, boil water, add orzo, and cook for 8 minutes; add in spinach, cook until it wilts, drains it, and set it aside.

- Add tomatoes in pork, add orzo, spinach mix. Sprinkle cheese and serve.

Nutrition per serving: 1-1/3 cups: calories 372|306mg sodium| 11g fat |2g sugars |4g saturated fat| 71mg cholesterol |3g fiber|31g protein|| 34g carbohydrate

4. Sesame Chicken with Couscous

Preparation time: 10 minutes

Cook time: 25 minutes

Total time: 35 minutes

Serving: 4

Ingredients:

- 1 and a half cups of water
- Cooked chicken breast, shredded: 2 cups
- Extra virgin olive oil: 1 tablespoon
- Whole-wheat couscous, uncooked: 1 cup
- Coleslaw mix: 2 cups
- Minced fresh cilantro: 2 tablespoons
- Chopped peanuts, it is optional
- Four sliced green onions
- Sesame salad, toasted dressing, low fat: 2 tablespoons+ ½ cup divided

Instructions:

- In a pan, boil water and add couscous. Let it simmer for 5 to 10 minutes until water is absorbed. Fluff it with a spoon.

- In a pan, add oil, coleslaw mix, and cook for 3 to 4 minutes, until soft.

- Add couscous, 2 tbsp. of dressing, and green onions, heat it through.

- Turn off the heat.

- In the same pan, add remaining dressing and chicken, cook on medium flame until all heated through.

- Serve with couscous, garnish with peanuts, cilantro.

Nutrition per serving: one cup of couscous + ½ cup of the chicken mixture without peanuts: 320 calories| 5g fiber|9g fat |1g saturated fat| 35g carbohydrate|54mg cholesterol| 9g sugars|26g protein|442mg sodium|

5. Chicken Stew

Preparation time: 10 minutes

Cook time: 5 hours

Total time: 5 hours & 10 minutes

Serving: 10

Ingredients:

- Sliced celery: 1 cup
- Skinless, boneless chicken breasts: 2 pounds, cut into one-inch cubes
- Peeled potatoes: 3 cups, cut into cubes
- Diced onion: 1 cup

- Coldwater: 1/4 cup

- Carrots: cut into thin slices, 1 cup

- 2 cans of (14 and a half ounces each) chicken broth, reduced-sodium

- 1 can of (6 ounces) tomato paste, no-salt-added

- Pepper: half teaspoon

- Half teaspoon of dried sage

- Corn-starch: 3 tablespoons

- Dried thyme: half teaspoon

- Paprika: 1 teaspoon

- Parmesan cheese, Shredded, it is optional

Instructions:

- In a slow cooker, add all ingredients except for corn-starch and water. Cover it and cook for four hours on high

- Mix corn-starch with water and add it to the stew. Cover and cook for half an hour, till vegetables, are soft.

- Serve with grated cheese.

Nutrition per serving: 1 cup: 180 calories|18g carbohydrate | 1g saturated fat| 2g fiber| 50mg cholesterol| 21g protein|280mg sodium| 4g sugars|2g fat |

6. Herb-Roasted Chicken Breasts

Preparation time: 10 minutes

Cook time: 30 minutes

Total time:40 minutes

Serving: 4-5

Ingredients:

- One onion
- 4 cups of chicken breasts (boneless and skinless)
- 1–2 cloves of garlic
- Ground black pepper: 1 teaspoon
- Olive oil: ¼ cup
- Garlic & Herb Seasoning: 2 tablespoons (no salt added)

Instructions:

- In a bowl, chop garlic, onion, add herb seasoning, olive oil, and pepper.
- Add chicken to this mix, cover with plastic wrap, then chill in the fridge for four hours.
- Let the oven preheat to 350 F

- Place marinated chicken on foil on a baking tray

- Add the marinade over chicken and bake for 20 minutes

- For browning, Broil for five minutes.

Nutrition Per Serving: Calories 270 | total Fat 17 g| Saturated Fat 3 g| Trans Fat 0 g| Cholesterol 83 mg| Sodium 53 mg| Carbohydrates 3 g| Protein 26 g| Phosphorus 252 mg| Potassium 491 mg| Dietary Fiber 0.6 g| Calcium 17 mg

7. Turmeric Lime Chicken

Preparation time: 10 minutes

Cook time: 30 minutes

Total time: 40 minutes

Serving: 6

Ingredients:

- Vegetable oil: 4-5 TBSP
- Three minced garlic cloves
- Turmeric: one tablespoon
- Cilantro: two tablespoons
- Two beaten egg whites
- Boneless chicken breasts: six (not thick)
- Four halved juicy limes
- Bread crumbs: 2 cups
- Salt and pepper to taste

Instructions:

- Make four tiny cuts on top of each chicken breast, then season on both sides with pepper and salt. This scoring will help the marinade flavours absorb the meat quicker and enable the chicken breasts to cook quicker and evenly.

- In a large bowl, combine fresh lime juice, minced garlic,

and chopped cilantro and put the mixture's chicken breasts. Cover it up, and let stay at room temperature for half an hour.

- Whisk the eggs. Combine the turmeric powder and the panko or bread crumbs in another container

- Put each breast of chicken in the beaten egg bowl and switch to cover with egg. Then cover the turmeric/bread crumb mixture on both sides of each chicken breast.

- Pan-fry the chicken breasts in a wide pan, use oil to coat the pan. Around 6-10 minutes per side, if required, after that, clean the pan. Repeat the process with each chicken breast.

- When the chicken is completely cooked, serve in a sandwich or with a delicious mango salsa, steamed or sautéed vegetables of your choosing.

Nutrition per serving: Calories 326 | Carbohydrates: 20g | Protein: 29g | Fat: 14g | Potassium 181mg| Phosphorus 102mg

Chapter 4: Fish & Seafood Recipes

1. Charred Shrimp & Pesto Buddha Bowls

Preparation time: 10 minutes

Cook time: 20 minutes

Total time: 30 minutes

Serving: 4

Ingredients:

- Pesto: 1/3 cup
- Vinegar: 2 tbsp.
- Olive oil: 1 tbsp.
- Salt: 1/4 tsp.
- Ground pepper: ¼ tsp.
- Peeled & deveined large shrimp: one pound
- Arugula: 4 cups
- Cooked quinoa: 2 cups

Instructions:

- In a large bowl, mix pesto, oil, vinegar, salt, and pepper. Take out four tbsp. of mixture in another bowl.
- Place skillet over medium flame. Add shrimp, let it cook

for five minutes, stirring, until only charred a little. move to a plate

- Use the vinaigrette to mix with quinoa and arugula in a bowl. Divide the mixture of the arugula into four bowls. Cover with shrimp, Add 1 tbsp. of the pesto mixture to each bowl. And serve.

Nutrition per Serving: 329 calories| total fat 18 g | carbohydrates 17.2 g| protein 17 g | Cholesterol 6.7 mg| Sodium 154 mg| potassium 143 mg| Phosphorus 123 mg |Calcium 45 mg| Fiber 2.1 g

2. Honey Spice-Rubbed Salmon

Preparation time: 10 minutes

Cook time: 20 minutes

Total time: 30 minutes

Serving: 4

Ingredients:

- 16 ounces of salmon fillets
- Honey: 3 tablespoons
- Half tsp. Of black pepper
- 2 pressed cloves of garlic
- Lemon peel: 3/4 teaspoon

- Hot water: 1 teaspoon

- Arugula: 3 cups

- Olive oil: 2 tablespoons

Instructions:

- In a bowl, add grated lemon peel, honey, hot water, ground pepper, garlic, and whisk well.

- With clean hands, rub the mixture over fish fillets.

- Over medium flame, heat the olive oil in a pan. Add marinated fish fillets and cook for four minutes. Turn once.

- Turn the heat to low and cook for 4-6 minutes or until fish is cooked through.

- Add half a cup of arugula to the plate. Put salmon fillet on arugula.

- Sprinkle with fresh herbs and serve.

Nutrition per serving: Calories 323 | Protein 23 g |Carbohydrates 15 g| Fat 19 g| Cholesterol 62 mg| Sodium 66 mg| Potassium 454 mg| Phosphorus 261 mg| Calcium 42 mg| Fiber 0.4 g

3. One-Sheet Roasted Garlic Salmon & Broccoli

Preparation time: 10 minutes

Cook time: 20 minutes

Total time: 30 minutes

Serving: 4

Ingredients:

- One head of broccoli cut into florets:3-4 cups
- Olive oil: 2 and a half tbsp.
- Salmon fillets (4 portions): 1 half pounds
- Two cloves of minced garlic
- Black pepper to taste
- Lemon slices

Instructions:

- Let the oven pre-heat to 450 F and line parchment paper on a baking sheet
- Put the pieces of salmon on the baking sheet, with spaces in between
- Three spray one tablespoon of oil over the fish Place the minced cloves of garlic thinly over the salmon.
- Add salt (if you want, few pinches) and ground black pepper to sprinkle over salmon. Finally, place the cut lemon on top of the salmon. set aside
- Then, mix 1and half tablespoons of oil, half a teaspoon of

salt, and ground black pepper in a medium bowl with the broccoli florets.

- Toss the florets. Arrange the broccoli around the salmon bits into the baking dish.

- Bake in the oven for fifteen minutes, until the fish is cooked through and the broccoli florets at the ends are slightly brown.

- Sprinkle with parsley for a garnish and, if needed, layer lemon slices around. Enjoy warm.

Nutrition per serving: Calories 256|Protein 12.3 g |Carbohydrates 9.2 g| Fat 11 g| Cholesterol 12 mg| Sodium 154 mg| potassium 187 mg| Phosphorus 145 mg |Calcium 75 mg| Fiber 2.5 g

4. Crunchy Oven-Fried Catfish

Preparation time: 10 minutes

Cook time: 20 minutes

Total time: 30 minutes

Serving: 4

Ingredients:

- Catfish fillets: 1 pound

- One egg white

- Cornmeal: 1/4 cup

- Panko bread crumbs: 1/4 cup

- Half cup all-purpose flour

- Cajun seasoning(salt-free): 1 teaspoon

Instructions:

- Let the oven preheat to 450 F.

- Spray oil on a baking tray.

- In a mixer, whisk the egg until soft peak forms.

- Add flour on parchment paper. On another sheet of parchment, mix the Cajun seasoning, cornmeal, and panko.

- Slice the fish into four fillets.

- Coat the fillet in flour, then in egg white, then in cornmeal mix.

- Dip the fish in the flour and shake off excess.

- Place the coated fish on a baking pan.

- Spray the fish fillets with cooking spray.

- Bake for 10 to 12 minutes, turn the fish over and bake for another five minutes.

- Serve hot

Nutrition per serving: Calories 250| Protein 22 g| Carbohydrates 19 g| Fat 10 g| Cholesterol 53 mg| Sodium 124 mg| Potassium 401 mg| Phosphorus 262 mg| Calcium 26 mg| Fiber 1.2 g

5. Grilled Blackened Tilapia

Preparation time: 10 minutes

Cook time: 20 minutes

Total time: 30 minutes

Serving: 4

Ingredients:

- Olive oil: 2 tablespoons

- Four tilapia filets

- Dried oregano: 1 teaspoon

- Half teaspoon. Of cayenne pepper

- 2 cloves of minced garlic

- Smoked paprika: 2 teaspoons

- Cumin: 3/4 teaspoon

Instructions:

- Preheat the grill on medium heat spray oil on the grill.

- Mix all the seasoning and coat the fish.

- Grill for almost three minutes on each side, or until cooked through

- Top with cilantro and serve

Nutrition per serving: calories 234 |Total Fat 9.3g| Cholesterol 58mg| Sodium 62.4mg| Total Carbohydrate 1.8g| Dietary Fiber 0.8g| Protein 23.7g| Iron 1.4mg| Potassium 403mg| Phosphorus 207.3mg|

Chapter 5: Appetizer, Sides & Snacks Recipes

1. Gluten-Free Hummus

Preparation time: 10 minutes

Cook time: 25 minutes

Total time: 35 minutes

Serving: 6

Ingredients:

- 2 garlic cloves
- Dried chickpeas: 2/3 cup cleaned, rinsed, and soaked overnight, drained
- 3 cups of water

- One bay leaf
- 3/4 cup+2 tablespoons of green onion, cut into slices
- 1/8 teaspoon of salt
- Fresh cilantro chopped: 3 tablespoons
- Extra virgin olive oil: 1 tablespoon
- Ground cumin: 1 teaspoon
- Sherry vinegar: 2 tablespoons

Instructions:

- In a pan, add water, bay leaf, chickpeas, a pinch of salt, garlic, cloves, and medium heat.
- Let it boil. Turn the heat low, cover it partially, let it simmer till the beans are soft, for 50-60 minutes.
- Take out the bay leaf and drain—Reserve half a cup of liquid and garlic.
- In a food processor, add the olive oil, chickpeas, garlic, remaining salt, vinegar, cumin, 3/4 cup of sliced green onion, and cumin.
- Pulse on high until pureed.
- Add one tbsp. of revered liquid at a time until the mixture has become thick.
- In a bowl, add hummus and mix with 2 tbsp. of green onion. Serve right away or serve chilled with pita chips.

Nutrition per serving: 1/4 cup: Calories 116|Total carbohydrate 15 g| Dietary fiber 4 g| Saturated fat 0.5 g| Sodium 210 mg| Total fat 4 g| Cholesterol 0 mg| Monounsaturated fat 2 g| Total sugars 3 g| Protein 5 g|

2. Fresh Fruit Kebabs

Preparation time: 10 minutes

Cook time: 25 minutes

Total time: 35 minutes

Serving: 2

Ingredients:

- Fresh lime juice: 1 teaspoon
- Lime zest: 1 teaspoon
- Half banana, cut into 4 and half-inch chunks
- 6 ounces of sugar-free, low-fat lemon yogurt
- 4 pineapple chunks, cut into half-inch of thickness
- Four strawberries
- Four wooden skewers, soaked in water
- One kiwi, quartered, peeled
- Four red grapes

Instructions:

- In a bowl, mix lime juice, zest, and yogurt. Cover it and keep it in the fridge.
- Add to skewers fruit of each kind, thread all the skewers until all fruits are used.
- Serve with lime lemon lime dip.

Nutrition per serving: 2 skewers of fruit kebabs: Calories 190| Total carbohydrate 39 mg| Total fat 2 g| Monounsaturated fat Trace| Saturated fat 1 g| Cholesterol 5 mg| Dietary fiber 4 g| Added sugars 6 g| Sodium 53 mg| Protein 4 g

3. Ginger-Marinated Grilled Portobello Mushrooms

Preparation time: 10 minutes

Cook time: 25 minutes

Total time: 35 minutes

Serving: 4

Ingredients:

- Four Portobello mushrooms, large-sized, cleaned and trimmed

- Balsamic vinegar: 1/4 cup

- Fresh basil, chopped: 1 tablespoon

- Pineapple juice: half cup

- Peeled fresh ginger: 2 tablespoons, chopped

Instructions:

- In a bowl, mix the pineapple juice, balsamic vinegar, and ginger.

- In a glass dish, place mushrooms, cut the stems, stemless side up. Pour over mushrooms.

- Cover it and let it marinate in the fridge for one hour, turn the mushroom halfway.

- Preheat the grill, spray the grill with oil, 4-6 inches away from the heat source.

- Broil or grill mushroom for five minutes on every side, until soft, turn often.

- Keep basting with the marinade so they would not dry out.

- Take mushroom out on a serving plate. Top with basil and serve right away.

Nutrition per serving: one mushroom: Calories 60| Cholesterol 0 mg| Sodium 15 mg| Total fat Trace| Total carbohydrate 12 g| Saturated fat Trace| Protein 3 g| Added sugars 0 g| Total sugars 8 g| Dietary fiber 2 g| Monounsaturated fat Trace|

4. Chickpea Polenta with Olives

Preparation time: 10 minutes

Cook time: 30 minutes

Total time: 40 minutes

Serving: 8

Ingredients:

For polenta:

- Half tablespoon of extra-virgin olive oil

- 1 and 3/4 cups of chickpea flour

- Plain soy milk: 2 cups

- Dry mustard: 1 teaspoon

- Chicken stock: 1 cup no sodium

- 3 cloves of minced garlic

- 3 large egg whites

- Chopped fresh thyme: 1 tablespoon, or oregano, basil

- Freshly ground black pepper: 1/4 teaspoon

For toppings:

- Half tablespoon of extra-virgin olive oil

- Parmesan cheese, grated: 2 tablespoons

- Half of the yellow onion, chopped

- Sun-dried tomatoes, dry-packed: 1/4 cup, soaked in water, drained and diced

- Fresh flat-leaf parsley, finely chopped: 2 tablespoons

- Roughly chopped: 1/4 cup pitted Kalamata olives

Instructions:

- In a food processor, add soy milk, olive oil, black pepper, stock, flour, mustard, thyme, and garlic.

- Pulse on high until smooth. Take out into a large bowl.

- Keep in the fridge for one hour.

- Let the oven preheat to 425 F. spray oil on a 9x13 baking dish.

- In an electric mixer, whisk the egg whites until stiff peaks form. Fold egg whites in the batter.

- Pour batter into prepared dish. Bake for 15 minutes, until slightly browned and puffy.

- Let it cool for 15 minutes.

- Let the broiler heat, place the rack 4 inch away from the heat source.

- In a pan, add olive oil, sauté onion over medium flame until lightly golden and soft, for six minutes.

- Add the tomatoes, olives, cook for one minute. Turn off the heat.

- Place cooked onion mix on top of baked polenta, top with cheese, and broil until it becomes lightly browned, for only one minute. Garnish with parsley.

- Cool for ten minutes, and slice into 8 pieces. Further, cut into more pieces.

- Serve right away.

Nutrition per serving: 2 wedges: Calories 157| Total carbohydrate 20 g| Total fat 5 g| Dietary fiber 3 g| Saturated fat 1 g| Sodium 160 mg| Monounsaturated fat 2 g| Cholesterol 2 mg |Protein 8 g| total sugars 4 g

Chapter 6: Vegetarian & Meatless Recipes

1. Spinach, Mushroom & Mozzarella Wraps

Preparation time: 10 minutes

Cook time: 30 minutes

Total time: 40 minutes

Serving: 4

Ingredients:

- Extra virgin olive oil: 1 tablespoon
- 2 and a half cups of fresh mushrooms, cut into slices
- Half pound of fresh arugula or spinach, trimmed and

steamed

- Minced garlic: 1 teaspoon

- 1 tomato, plum, finely diced

- 2, 8-inch tortillas: whole wheat

- ¼ cup of (1 ounce) mozzarella cheese, part-skim, shredded

Instructions:

- Let the oven preheat to 350 F

- In a pan, add one tbsp. of olive oil, on medium flame.

- Add garlic and mushroom slices in one even layer, let them sauté, do not stir, turn them once as the other side also develops brown color.

- Lay tortilla flat, add a steamed spinach layer and then add tomatoes, cheese, and sautéed mushrooms.

- Roll tightly and put seam side down on baking dish (greased slightly)

- Bake for ten minutes, until cheese melts.

- Cut the tortillas in quarters. Serve hot and enjoy.

Nutrition per serving: About half tortilla: Calories 78| Total carbohydrate 12 g| Sodium 46 mg| Total fat 3g| Trans-fat 0 g| Saturated fat Trace| Cholesterol 0.9 g| Dietary fiber 4 g| Monounsaturated fat 0.8 g| Added sugars 0 g| Protein 7 g|

2. Soba Noodles with Mushroom, Spinach & Tofu

Preparation time: 10 minutes

Cook time: 35 minutes

Total time: 45 minutes

Serving: 4-6

Ingredients:

- 2 cloves of minced garlic
- 1 carrot, medium-sized finely diced
- 1 cup of frozen edamame, thawed
- 1 and a half Tbsp. of finely minced fresh ginger
- One and a half cup of brown or white mushrooms, cut into slices
- 1 shallot, small-sizes minced
- 2 Tbsp. of extra virgin olive oil
- 1 and a half cups of chicken broth, low-sodium, or vegetable broth
- 6 oz. of soba noodles

- 2 Tbsp. of soy sauce, reduced-sodium

- 1 tsp. of lemon zest, grated

- 1/4 tsp. of freshly ground black pepper

- Half cup of spinach leaves, chopped

- Half cup of firm tofu, diced into half-inch of thickness

Instructions:

- In a large pot, add water, let it boil

- In a pan, add olive oil, sauté garlic, shallot, ginger, and carrots on a medium flame for one minute.

- Add in mushrooms, turn the flame to low, and cover the pan. Let the mushroom becomes soft for about four minutes.

- Take off the cover, and turn the flame to medium-high.

- Add in edamame and cook for 2 minutes, until heated through. Add in soy sauce, broth, and lemon zest. Mix well and let it boil.

- Add in spinach, cook until wilted. Add in tofu, take off from the heat. Taste and add black pepper to your liking.

- Cook soba noodles by dropping in boiling water, cook to your preference, for about five minutes. Drain and wash with cool water.

- Add cooked pasta to the pan on medium flame. Mix the noodles with cooked vegetables. Heat it through. Serve in bowls.

Nutrition per serving: About one cup: Calories 154| Total carbohydrate 13 g| Sodium 56 mg| Total fat 3.4 g| Trans-fat 0 g| Saturated fat Trace| Cholesterol 2 g| Dietary fiber 5 g| Monounsaturated fat 0.2 g| Added sugars 0 g| Protein 5 g|

3. Vegetable Pasta Soup

Preparation time: 10 minutes

Cook time: 35 minutes

Total time: 45 minutes

Serving: 12

Ingredients:

- Extra virgin olive oil: 2 teaspoons

- 6 cloves of minced garlic

- Snipped fresh parsley: 2 tablespoons

- 1 and a half cups of roughly shredded carrot

- 1 cup of celery, cut into thin slices

- 4 cups of chicken broth, reduced-sodium

- 1/4 cup of Parmesan cheese, grated

- 4 cups of water

- 1 and a half cups of dried Ditalini pasta

- 1 cup of chopped onion

Instructions:

- In a large Dutch oven, add olive oil, garlic, and cook for 15 seconds on medium flame.

- Add celery, carrot, and onion, cook for 5-7 minutes or until soft, stirring occasionally. Add water and chicken broth, let it boil. Add uncooked Ditalini pasta, cook for 7 - 8 minutes, or until pasta is al dente.

- Pour into bowls, top with parsley and grated cheese.

Nutrition per serving: About one cup: Calories 88| Total carbohydrate 9 g| Sodium 45 mg| Total fat 3g| Trans-fat 0 g| Saturated fat Trace| Cholesterol 01 g| Dietary fiber 4.6 g| Monounsaturated fat 0.8 g| Added sugars 0 g| Protein 7.3 g|

4. Gazpacho with Chickpeas

Preparation time: 10 minutes

Cook time: 60-70 minutes

Total time: 80 minutes

Serving: 6

Ingredients:

- Half cup of chopped, remove seeds, cucumber
- 1 can of (15 ounces) chickpeas, drained and rinsed
- 1 cup of cherry tomatoes, cut into quarters
- 1/4 cup of finely chopped red onion
- 6 cups of unsalted homemade vegetable juice
- 1 to 3 cloves of garlic minced
- 1/4 cup of finely chopped fresh parsley or cilantro
- 1/4 cup of fresh lime juice
- 6 lime cut into wedges
- 1/4 teaspoon of hot pepper sauce

Instructions:

- In a big bowl, add tomatoes, chickpeas, cilantro, vegetable juice, hot pepper sauce, lime juice, cucumber, garlic, and onions. Mix well.

- Cover with plastic wrap and keep in the refrigerator for one hour or more.

- For serving, add cold soup in bowls, top with cilantro and lime wedges.

- Serve right away.

Nutrition per serving: About one and a half cups: Calories 125| Total carbohydrate 24 g| Sodium 156 mg| Dietary fiber 5 g| Saturated fat Trace| Cholesterol 0 mg| Protein 7 g| Total fat 1 g| Total sugars 8 g| Monounsaturated fat 0.5 g| Trans-fat 0 g|

5. Wild Rice Pilaf with Cranberries & Apples

Preparation time: 10 minutes

Cook time: 35 minutes

Total time: 45 minutes

Serving: 8

Ingredients:

- 3 cups of water
- Extra virgin olive oil: 2 tablespoons
- 1 and a half cups of wild rice, rinsed & drained
- Half cup of no sugar added dried cranberries
- 2 tart apples, core removed and diced

- 1/4 cup of slivered almonds
- Red wine vinegar: 1 tablespoon
- 1 tablespoon honey

Instructions:

- Let the oven preheat to 325 F.
- On a baking sheet, spray with cooking spray.
- Place almonds on the greased baking sheet, bake until golden, often stirring, for ten minutes.
- Take out in a bowl, let them cool.
- In a pan, add three cups of water, add rice. Cover and turn the heat to low—Cook for 45-60 minutes. Keep adding more water so that the rice won't dry out.
- Strain through fine-mesh. Add back to the pan, and add dried cranberries.
- Cover it and set it aside.
- In a bowl, mix honey, oil, and vinegar.
- In another bowl, add the apple and rice. Pour over oil mixture, coat evenly.
- Serve cold or warm. Garnish with toasted almonds.

Nutrition per serving: About one cup: 213 Calories | Total carbohydrate 37 g| Total fat 5 g| Saturated fat 1 g| Sodium 6 mg| Monounsaturated fat 4 g| Cholesterol 0 mg| added sugars 4 g| Protein 5 g| Dietary fiber 4 g|

6. Thyme Roasted Beets

Preparation time: 10 minutes

Cook time: 35 minutes

Total time: 45 minutes

Serving: 4

Ingredients:

- Extra virgin olive oil: 1 tablespoon
- 1/4 teaspoon of freshly ground black pepper
- 1 teaspoon of fresh thyme
- 1/8 teaspoon of salt
- 2 medium-sized, red or golden beets, cleaned and trimmed

Instructions:

- Let the oven preheat to 400 F.
- Wrap the beets in foil and bake for 40 minutes or more until they become soft.
- Cool them slightly. Peel and cut the beets into normal-sized chunks.
- In a bowl, add pieces of beets, salt, oil, pepper, and thyme. Coat well
- Put on a baking sheet and bake for 5-10 minutes, until hot.

Nutrition per serving: half of a cup: Calories 59| Total carbohydrate 7 g| Total fat 3 g| Trans-fat 0 g| Monounsaturated fat 2 g| Saturated fat 0 g| Cholesterol 0 mg| Dietary fiber 2 g| Total sugars 5 g| Sodium 126 mg| Protein 1 g

Chapter 7: Soups & Salad Recipes

1. Turkey, Wild Rice, & Mushroom Soup

Preparation time: 10 minutes

Cook time: 45 minutes

Total time: 55 minutes

Serving: 4-5

Ingredients:

- Turkey: 2 cups, cooked, shredded
- Half cup of onion, chopped
- Half cup of carrots, chopped
- Two garlic cloves, minced
- Chicken broth, low-sodium: 5 cups
- Half cup of red bell pepper, chopped
- Half cup of uncooked wild rice,
- Olive oil: 1 tablespoon
- Half teaspoon salts
- Two bay leaves
- Herb seasoning: 1/4 teaspoon

- Dried thyme: 1-and half teaspoon

- Black pepper: 1/4 teaspoon

- Half cup of sliced mushrooms

Instructions:

- In a pot, boil the one and ¾ broth over medium flame. Add rice to the broth and cook. Let it boil. Turn the heat down. Cover it and let it simmer until all broth is absorbed.

- In a Dutch oven, heat oil, add garlic, bell pepper, onion, and carrots. Sauté them.

- Add the mushroom to the vegetables, then add the broth, turkey, herb seasoning, salt, pepper, thyme, and bay leaves. Cook until it is well heated. Stir often.

- Before adding the rice, take out the bay leaves. Cook for a minute and serve.

Nutrition per serving: Calories 210| Protein 23 g| Carbohydrates 15 g| Fat 5 g| Cholesterol 35 mg| Sodium 270 mg| Potassium 380 mg| Phosphorus 200 mg| Calcium 32 mg| Fiber 2.3 g

2. Lemon Chicken Soup

Preparation time: 10 minutes

Cook time: 35 minutes

Total time: 45 minutes

Serving: 4

Ingredients:

- Eggs: 3 large whites
- Chicken broth: 6 cups
- Shredded and cooked chicken breast:1 cup
- Fresh lemon juice:1/4 cup

- Kosher Salt and freshly ground black pepper (to taste.)

- Orzo:1 cup

Instructions:

- Add chicken stock to a big saucepan and let it boil.

- Add in orzo, cook until soft to your liking.

- Mix the eggs and lemon juice.

- When orzo is cooked to your liking, take out one cup of chicken broth and add in egg mix one tablespoon at a time. Mixing constantly

- Then add this egg mixture back into the broth, constantly stirring.

- Add the cooked shredded chicken in the broth, let it simmer until the soup becomes thick, often stirring, for about five minutes.

- Add salt and freshly ground black pepper to taste.

Nutrition per serving: Calories 451|Carbs: 42g| Protein: 32g |Fat: 15g||Sodium 212 mg | Phosphorus 32 mg| Calcium 36 mg | Potassium 156 mg|

3. Vegan Minestrone Soup

Preparation time: 10 minutes

Cook time: 35 minutes

Total time: 45 minutes

Serving: 6

Ingredients:

- Cubed bread: one cup

- Low-sodium vegetable broth: 3 cups

- Garlic: 5 cloves

- Leek: one cup (chopped)

- Olive oil: 3 tbsp.

- Carrots: one cup(chopped)

- Water: three cups

- Small pasta: one cup

- Kosher salt: 3/4 tsp.

- Beans: 15 ounces

- Baby kale: 3 cups

- Zucchini: 10 ounces (thinly sliced)

- Peas: 1 cup

- Ground pepper: half teaspoon

Instructions:

- Let the oven Preheat oven to 350 F.

- Cook the garlic in two tablespoons of oil over medium heat in a medium skillet, stirring continuously for three minutes until the garlic is softened.

- Add bread; toss it to coat. Spread the combination uniformly on a baking dish. Bake, for ten minutes, until toasted.

- In the meanwhile, heat the leftover one tablespoon oil over medium flame in a big pan. Add the leek and carrots; simmer for five minutes, stirring frequently until softened.

- Add salt, broth, and water, cover it and bring to a simmer over a high flame.

- Add the pasta on low flame; cook uncovered for five minutes, stirring regularly. Then add zucchini, stirring regularly, for around five minutes, until the pasta is al dente.

- Stir in kale, beans, peas, and seasoning. Cook for around two minutes, stirring regularly until the kale is wilted.

- Pour the soup into six bowls, evenly garnish with the croutons.

Nutrition per serving: Calories 267 | total fat 8.6g |carbohydrates 8.7g | protein 9.7g |sodium 67 mg

4. Yucatan Lime Soup

Preparation time: 10 minutes

Cook time: 40 minutes

Total time: 50 minutes

Serving: 2-3

Ingredients:

- Eight cloves of garlic, minced
- Chicken breast: 1 and a half cups cooked, shredded
- Two serrano chili peppers, chopped
- Chicken broth, low-sodium: 4 cups
- One small tomato

- Cilantro: 1/4 cup, chopped

- Half cup of onion, diced

- Two tortillas, cut into strips

- Olive oil: 1 tablespoon

- 1/4 teaspoon of salt

- Black pepper

- 1 bay leaf

- Lime juice: 1/4 cup

Instructions:

- Let the oven preheat to 400° F.

- place tortilla strips on a baking tray and spray with oil. Bake for three minutes or till slightly toasted. Take out from the oven and set it aside.

- In a pot, sauté chili, garlic, and onion in olive oil, till translucent

- Add salt, chicken, tomato, bay leaf, and chicken. Simmer for ten minutes.

- Add black pepper, cilantro, lime juice.

- Serve with toasted strips.

Nutrition per serving: Calories 214| Protein 20 g| Carbohydrates 12 g| Fat 10 g| Cholesterol 32 mg| Sodium 246 mg| Potassium 355 mg| Phosphorus 176 mg| Calcium 47 mg| Fiber 1.6 g

5. Low Sodium Chicken Soup

Preparation time: 10 minutes

Cook time: 50 minutes

Total time: 60 minutes

Serving: 4

Ingredients:

- Onion: 1 tablespoon
- Mixed vegetables: 1 cup
- 4 cups of chicken breast cooked, shredded
- Four stalks of celery, chopped
- Carrots: 1 cup, chopped
- Butter: 1 tablespoon
- Chicken broth, low-sodium: 5 cups
- Fresh parsley: 2 tablespoons
- Seven and a half cups water
- Black pepper: 1/8 teaspoon

Instructions:

- In a large pot, sauté onion in butter for five minutes.
- Add chicken broth and water let it boil.
- Add parsley, chicken, pepper, celery, cover it and let it simmer for half an hour.

- Add carrots, simmer for 20 minutes, then add frozen vegetables cook for another 20 minutes.

- Serve hot.

Nutrition per serving: Calories 97| Protein 13 g| Carbohydrates 5 g| Fat 3 g| Cholesterol 31 mg| Sodium 301 mg| Potassium 274 mg| Phosphorus 116 mg| Calcium 27 mg| Fiber 1.6 g

6. Slow-Cooker Chicken & Chickpea Soup

Preparation time: 10 minutes

Cook time: 4-8 hours and 10 minutes

Total time: 4-8 hours and 20 minutes

Serving: 5-6

Ingredients:

- 8 cups bone-in, trimmed skin removed, chicken thighs,
- Dried chickpeas: 1 and a ½ cups (soaked overnight)
- Chopped red bell pepper: 1 and a half cup
- One large yellow onion, thinly sliced
- Tomato paste: 2 tablespoons
- 4 cups of water
- 4 cloves of garlic, minced
- One bay leaf
- Paprika: 4 teaspoons
- Ground cumin: 4 teaspoons
- ¼ of a teaspoon freshly ground black pepper
- ¼ of a cup halved pitted olives(oil-cured)
- Half of a teaspoon salt
- ¼ of a cup of chopped fresh parsley
- ¼ of a teaspoon cayenne pepper

Instructions:

- Rinse and drain the chickpeas, put them in a large slow cooker, add four cups of water, chopped red pepper, bay leaf, tomato paste, and paprika cayenne, freshly ground black pepper, garlic, cumin.

- Mix well then, add the chicken.

- Cover it and cook on High for four hours or on low for at least 8 hours.

- Take out the chicken to a cutting surface and let it cool a little.

- Throw away the bay leaf. Then add olives, salt to the cooker and mix well.

- With forks, shred the chicken, set aside the bones. You would not need them.

- Add the shredded chicken into the soup.

- Garnish with cilantro and parsley.

- Serve hot.

Nutrition per serving: Calories 446 | total fat 15.3g |carbohydrates 43g |protein 21.6g |Cholesterol 22.3 mg| Sodium 221 mg| Potassium 332 mg| Phosphorus 187 mg| Calcium 24 mg| Fiber 2.8 g

Chapter 8: Desserts Recipes

1. Mixed Berry Pie

Preparation time: 10 minutes

Cook time: 30 minutes

Total time: 40 minutes

Serving: 6

Ingredients:

- Sugar-free, fat-free, vanilla pudding, instantly made: half cup, make sure it is made with fat-free milk
- 3/4 cup of fresh raspberries
- For garnish, 7 fresh mint leaves
- 6 single-serve of graham cracker in pie crusts
- 12 to 15 medium-sized strawberries, cut into slices, about ¾ of a cup
- Light whipped topping: 6 tablespoons

Instructions:

- Cook the vanilla fat-free pudding as per instruction on the package.
- In a bowl, add raspberries and slices of strawberries. Mix well.
- Add four tsp of pudding to every pie crust.

- Add 2 tbsp. of berry mixture in every pie crust. Add one tbsp. of light whipped topping.

- Place fresh mint leaves on top.

- Serve right away or keep in the refrigerator to chill until ready to serve.

Nutritional per serving: Serving size: one pie: Calories 133| Cholesterol 0.5 mg| Total carbohydrate 20 g| Protein 2 g| Dietary fiber 2 g| Added sugars 5.1 g |Monounsaturated fat 1.5 g| Trans-fat 0 g| Sodium 169 mg| Saturated fat 3 g| Total sugars 8 g|

2. Peach Crumble

Preparation time: 10 minutes

Cook time: 50 minutes

Total time: 60 minutes

Serving: 8

Ingredients:

- 8 peaches, ripe and peeled, remove seed and cut into slices
- 1/4 cup of dark brown sugar, packed
- 1/3 teaspoon of ground cinnamon
- Fresh Juice from 1 lemon
- 1/4 teaspoon of ground nutmeg
- Trans-free margarine, 2 tablespoons, thinly sliced
- Whole-wheat flour: half cup
- Quick-cooking oats: 1/4 cup uncooked

Instructions:

- Let the oven preheat to 375 F. take a 9" pie pan, spray with cooking spray.
- Add slices of peach to the pie pan—drizzle lemon juice on top, nutmeg, and cinnamon.
- In a bowl, add brown sugar and flour, mix well. With clean hands, add margarine to sugar-flour mixture. Add oats (uncooked) and mix well.

- Add flour mix on all over peach slices.

- Bake for half an hour, until peaches are tender and the top is brown.

- Cut into eight slices and serve right away.

Nutrition per serving: Serving size: one slice: Calories 152| Protein 3 g| Cholesterol 0 mg| Total fat 4 g| Total carbohydrate 26 g| Dietary fiber 3 g| Saturated fat 0.6 g| Sodium 41 mg| Monounsaturated fat 2 g| Added sugars 4 g

3. Poached Pears

Preparation time: 10 minutes

Cook time: 40 minutes

Total time: 50 minutes

Serving: 4

Ingredients:

- 1 teaspoon of ground nutmeg
- 1 cup of fresh orange juice
- 1 teaspoon of ground cinnamon
- 4 whole pears
- 2 tablespoons of grated fresh orange zest
- Half cup of fresh raspberries
- 1/4 cup of unsweetened apple juice

Instructions:

- In a bowl, add nutmeg, juices, and cinnamon, whisk to combine.

- Peel and trim the pears, remove the core, and leave the stem.

- Put the pears in a pan. Add juice mix in the pan, on medium flame.

- Let it simmer for half an hour. Keep turning the pears.

Do not let it boil.

- Serve the poached pears with orange zest, raspberries on top.

- Serve right away and enjoy it.

Nutrition per serving: Serving size: one pear: Calories 140|Protein 1 g| Cholesterol 0 mg| Total fat 0.5 g| Total carbohydrate 34 g| Monounsaturated fat Trace| Added sugars 0 g | Dietary fiber 2 g| Saturated fat Trace| Trans-fat 0 g| Sodium 9 mg

4. Lemon Pudding Cakes

Preparation time: 10 minutes

Cook time: 30 minutes

Total time: 40 minutes

Serving: 6

Ingredients:

- 1/4 teaspoon of salt

- Unsalted melted butter: 1 tablespoon

- Skim milk: 1 cup

- 2 whole eggs

- Freshly squeezed lemon juice: 1/3 cup

- All-purpose flour: 3 tablespoons

- 3/4 cup of honey or sugar

- Finely grated lemon peel: 1 tablespoon

Instructions:

- Let the oven preheat to 350 F.

- Take six custard cups and spray with cooking oil.

- Take two bowls and add egg whites in one and egg yolk in the other bowl.

- With a stand mixer, whisk egg at high speed. Slowly add ¼ cup of sugar, whisk until stiff peaks form.

- With a stand mixer, whisk the egg yolks with ½ cup of sugar well sugar is incorporated, add lemon peel, milk, butter, flour, and lemon juice.

- Mix for 2-3 minutes until smooth.

- Fold the egg whites into egg yolks mix with a spatula. Do not over mixture.

- Pour mixture in custard cup only fill half of the cup.

- Place custard cups in a 13x9" baking dish, put in the oven.

- Add boiling water to a baking dish until water is halfway to the sides of custard cups.

- Bake for 40-45 minutes, until tops are firm and golden. Take out from the oven in a baking dish and let it cool on a wire rack.

- Serve and enjoy.

Nutrition per serving: Serving size: 1 cup of custard cup: Calories 174| Saturated fat 2 g| Sodium 124 mg| Trans-fat 0 g| Total fat 4 g| | Cholesterol 68 mg| Total carbohydrate 34 g| Dietary fiber 2 g| Total sugars 28 g| Protein 4 g|

Chapter 9: DASH Diet Bonus Recipes

1. Zucchini Pizza Boats

Preparation time: 10 minutes

Cook time: 35 Minutes

Total time: 45 minutes

Serving: 6

Ingredients:

- Half cup of tomato pasta sauce, low sodium

- 2 large zucchinis

- Half cup of shredded mozzarella cheese, reduced-fat

- Black pepper

- Parmesan cheese: 2 tablespoons

Instructions:

- Let the oven preheat to 350 F

- Wash and pat dry zucchinis, cut in half, with a spoon take out the soft middle part

- Add zucchinis to a baking dish, add tomato-based pasta sauce on top, sprinkle cheeses and black pepper.

- Bake for half an hour or until cooked through. Serve it warm.

Nutrition per serving: Calories: 181|Sugar: 3 g| Sodium: 89 mg| Fat: 9 g| Carbohydrates: 11 g| Protein: 13 g| Cholesterol: 4 mg|

2. Zucchini Pizza Bites

Preparation time: 10 minutes

Cook time: 10 Minutes

Total time: 20 minutes

Serving: 1

Ingredients:

- Four slices of large zucchini, cut into the ¼-inch thickness
- Pizza sauce: 4 tablespoons
- Olive oil spray
- Shredded skim mozzarella cheese: 2 tablespoons
- Black pepper

Instructions:

- Let the broiler preheat to 500 F
- On both sides of zucchini slices, spray olive oil, and sprinkle with black pepper.
- Keep in the broiler for two minutes on each side.
- Take out from the broiler and add one tbsp. of pizza sauce and some shredded cheese.

- Broil for another minute or until cheese melts.

- Serve right away and enjoy it.

Nutrition per serving: Calories: 213|Sugar: 8 g| Sodium: 108 mg| Fat: 9 g| Carbohydrates: 11.1 g| Protein: 12.1 g| Cholesterol: 4 mg|

3. Cheesesteak Quiche

Preparation time: 10 minutes

Cook time: 20 Minutes

Total time: 30 minutes

Serving: 4

Ingredients:

- Olive oil: 2 tablespoons
- 2 cups of trimmed sirloin steak, roughly chopped
- Onions: 1 cup, chopped
- Cheese: Half cup, shredded
- Six egg white whisked
- Ground black pepper: half teaspoon
- Low-fat Cream: 1 cup
- Par-cooked prepared piecrust

Instructions:

- In a pan with oil, Sauté onions, and chopped steak. Cook until meat is cooked. Let it cool for ten minutes. Mix in cheese set it aside.
- In a bowl, whisk cream eggs with black pepper, mix it well.

- Add cheese mix and steak on pie crust, then add the egg mixture on top and half an hour bake at 350° F.

- Turn off the oven and Cover the quiche with foil.

- Let it sit for ten minutes, then serve.

Nutrition Per Serving: Calories 527| Total Fat 19 g| Saturated Fat 17 g| Trans Fat 1 g| Cholesterol 240 mg| Sodium 392 mg| Carbohydrates 22 g| Protein 22 g| Phosphorus 281 mg| Potassium 308 mg| Dietary Fiber 1 g| Calcium 137 mg

4. Tofu Scrambler

Preparation time: 10 minutes

Cook time: 20 Minutes

Total time: 30 minutes

Serving: 2

Ingredients:

- Onion powder: 1 teaspoon
- Olive oil: 1 teaspoon
- Green bell pepper: ¼ cup diced
- Red bell pepper: ¼ cup diced
- Turmeric: ⅛ teaspoon
- Firm tofu: 1 cup (less than 10% calcium)
- 2 clove garlic, minced

Instructions:

- In a non-stick pan, add bell peppers and garlic in olive oil.
- Rinse the tofu, and add in skillet break it into pieces with hands.
- Add all the remaining ingredients.
- Stir often, and cook on medium flame until the tofu

becomes a light golden brown, for almost 20 minutes.

- Serve warm.

Nutrition Per Serving: Calories 213 Cal| Total Fat 13 g| Saturated Fat 2 g| Trans Fat 0 g| Cholesterol 0 mg| Sodium 24 mg| Carbohydrates 10 g |Protein 18 g| Phosphorus 242 mg| Potassium 467 mg| Dietary Fiber 2 g| Calcium 274 mg

Chapter 10: Sauces & Dressings

1. Avocado Salsa

Preparation time: 10 minutes

Cooking time: 0 minutes

Total time: 10 minutes

Servings: 4

Ingredients:

- 1 small yellow onion, minced
- 1 jalapeno, minced
- ¼ cup cilantro, chopped
- A pinch of black pepper
- 2 avocados, peeled, pitted and cubed
- 2 tablespoons lime juice

Instructions:

- In a bowl, combine the onion with the jalapeno, cilantro, black pepper, avocado and lime juice, toss and serve.
- Enjoy!

Nutrition per serving: Calories 198 g | Total fat 2 g | Total fiber 5 g | Total carbohydrate 14 g | Protein 7 g

2. Watermelon Tomato Salsa

Preparation time: 10 minutes

Cooking time: 0 minutes

Total time: 10 minutes

Servings: 16

Ingredients:
- 4 yellow tomatoes, seedless and chopped
- A pinch of black pepper
- 1 cup watermelon, seedless and chopped
- 1/3 cup red onion, chopped
- 2 jalapeno peppers, chopped
- ¼ cup cilantro, chopped
- 3 tablespoons lime juice

Instructions:
- In a bowl, mix tomatoes with watermelon, onion and jalapeno.
- Add cilantro, lime juice and pepper, toss, divide between plates and serve as a side dish.
- Enjoy!

Nutrition per serving: Calories 87 g | Total fat 1 g | Total fiber 2 g | Total carbohydrate 4 g | Protein 7 g

3. Simple Salsa

Preparation time: 10 minutes

Cooking time: 0 minutes

Total time: 10 minutes

Servings: 6

Ingredients:

- 1 yellow bell pepper, cubed

- 2 tomatoes cubed, 1 cucumber cubed

- 1 small red onion, cubed

- 1 tablespoon olive oil

- 1 tablespoon red vinegar

Instructions:

- In a bowl, combine the bell pepper with the tomatoes, cucumber, onion, oil and vinegar, toss, divide into small cups and serve.

- Enjoy!

Nutrition per serving: Calories 142 g | Total fat 4 g | Total fiber 4 g | Total carbohydrate 6 g | Protein 7 g

Conclusion

Food is a form of love- for me it is. That's why I want to personally thank you for reading my book.

This amazing lifestyle will change your life forever and it will transform you into a happier and healthier person in no time!

Eating good and healthy food is not only possible, it is also simple, you just need to know the food.

Eating is essential and science helps us to choose what to eat in order to keep healthy, but we must not forget that a healthy diet is also varied and appetizing. It can be the occasion for something good for oneself, not only from a strictly physical point of view: the occasion to experiment new flavors and to share with someone the pleasure of preparing and eating a tasty dish.

The purpose of this cookbook is precisely to combine these different aspects, providing dishes using fresh ingredients.

Enjoy your meal, but even before that, enjoy smart shopping and have fun in the kitchen!

CPSIA information can be obtained
at www.ICGtesting.com
Printed in the USA
LVHW080906220621
690766LV00002B/314

9 781914 129971